Marriage Is Not For Chickens

Dr. Margaret Rutherford

Photography by Christine Mathias and Deborah Strauss

12
Things
Marriage is Not

Marriage is not for chickens.
It's hard work.

Marriage is not a dictatorship. You don't want to win all the time, because that would mean your partner would lose all the time.

Marriage is not rocket science. The principles are simple: respect, kindness, and loyalty.

Marriage
is not
old-
fashioned.

Marriage is not in and of itself stimulating. The two of you can get in a rut. You have to keep things fresh.

Marriage is not about collecting things. The joys of marriage aren't tangible.
You live them.

Marriage is not for the impatient.
Some of the best stuff takes a while to develop.
You have to stick around to find out.

Marriage is not the place for contempt.
That will ruin any chance of true intimacy and
dissolve the hope that once might have existed.

Marriage is not a 24-hour repair shop.
Your partner isn't supposed to meet your every
need. Some of those you have to take care of
through friendships or hobbies.

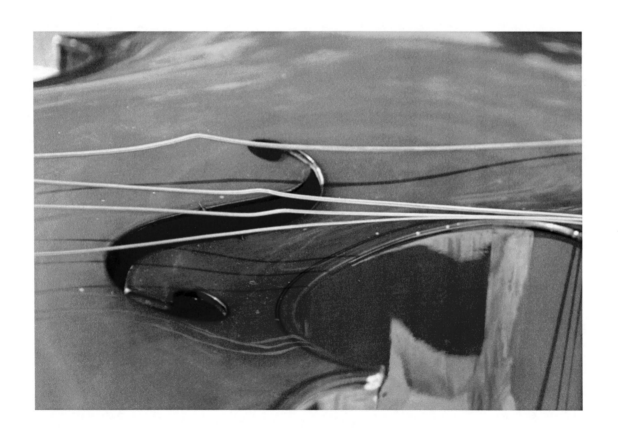

Marriage is not self-sustaining; it will not thrive on its own. If all you focus on is the kids, you are making a mistake.

Marriage is not boring. Two lives woven together can be exciting. There's something about watching someone very different from you live their life. You learn from that.

Marriage is not without conflict. Knowing how to disagree and work through anger and disappointment is key to feeling true closeness. Other relationships may end due to anger. Not marriage.

12 Things Marriage Is

Marriage is the potential for an intense, deep, and diverse intimacy.

Marriage is about
vulnerability.
Giving someone the
chance to hurt or
disappoint you, while
simultaneously giving
them the opportunity
to bring you
tremendous joy
and laughter.

Marriage is
trusting
someone
has your
back.
Always.

Marriage is
realizing that you
have been seen at
your worst times,
and are still loved.
You feel incredible
gratitude for that
gift, and give
it back.

Marriage is hearing the same story over and over, but every time, it makes you laugh so hard that you're left gasping for breath.

Marriage is thinking about the other one not
being there anymore.
And not being able to think about it.

Marriage is getting irritated by the things that always irritate you. Have irritated you for years. Will irritate you for many more. And tolerating them because they're way overbalanced by the good stuff.

Marriage is not being able to wait to get home to share some little something.

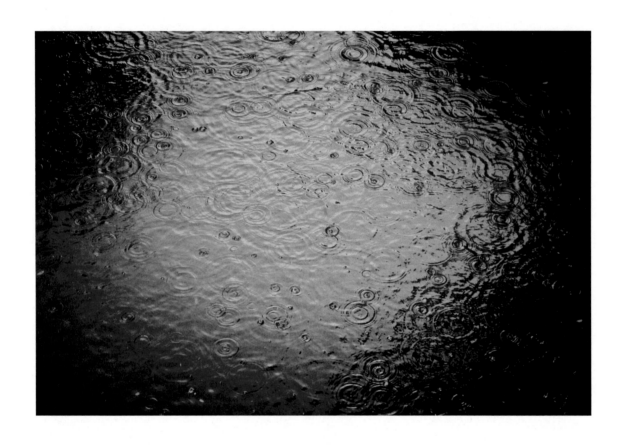

Marriage is getting teary-eyed together.

Marriage is about fighting more
fairly - learning how to apologize,
listen and to find resolution.

Marriage is
wishing you
were the one
having the
operation or
illness, not
your partner.

Marriage is a promise.
A vow - to try the hardest you have ever tried in
your life, for a chance to achieve a personal
integrity not found anywhere else.

Photography Legend

Christine Mathias' Photographs

Deborah Strauss' Photographs

About the Photographers

Deborah Strauss is a writer and photographer living is Austin, Texas. She particularly likes to capture the imperfectly perfect world that surrounds us all.

Christine Mathias has been a photographer since the days of film and darkrooms. She has had several one-person shows in California and Michigan, and her fine art is in private collections throughout the Unites States and as far away as the Middle East.

Made in the USA
San Bernardino, CA
23 June 2017